BOOKS BY LILIAN MOORE

Papa Albert
I Feel the Same Way
I Thought I Heard the City
Sam's Place
See My Lovely Poison Ivy
To See the World Afresh
(*Compiled by Lilian Moore and Judith Thurman*)

THINK OF SHADOWS

Think of
SHADOWS

poems by LILIAN MOORE

pictures by DEBORAH ROBISON

Atheneum *1980* *New York*

"Is There a Place?" first appeared in *See My Lovely Poison Ivy*
by Lilian Moore, published by Atheneum,
copyright © 1975.

LIBRARY OF CONGRESS CATALOGING IN PUBLICATION DATA

; *Moore, Lilian.*
Think of Shadows.

SUMMARY: *A collection of poems sharing shadows*
as a common theme.
1. Shades and shadows—Juvenile poetry.
2. Children's poetry, American. [1. Shades and
shadows—Poetry. 2. American poetry]
I. Robison, Deborah. II. Title.
PS3563.0622S5   811'.54   80-13496
ISBN 0-689-30782-9

Text copyright © 1975, 1980 by Lilian Moore
Illustrations copyright © 1980 by Deborah Robison
All rights reserved
Published simultaneously in Canada by
McClelland & Stewart, Ltd.
Printed by The Halliday Lithograph Corporation
West Hanover, Massachusetts
Bound by A. Horowitz & Sons/Bookbinders
Fairfield, New Jersey
Designed by Deborah Robison & M. M. Ahern
First Edition

To Stacy and Marc

&

To Stefan and Elizabeth

CONTENTS

THINK OF SHADOWS

WAKE UP, SHADOWS

The stars wink out.
They blink out
one by one.

The sky is pearly
now that night
is done.

The light gets bold,
grows gold—
here comes the sun!

Wake up, people.
Wake up, shadows.
Day's begun.

GREAT MOUSE

Hey, cat!
Pull in your
Claws,
Sheathe their fire.
Scat!
Your turn to tremble
In this
House.

Quick,
Great Mouse!
Before I run,
Before you
Fade,
Tell me
How it feels
To be so
Unafraid.

PARTNERS

This is the wind's doing,
this clothesline
dance—

shirttails twirling,
sleeves
clapping, thigh-slapping,
jeans stepping high.

What flapping, snapping,
whirling
to the wind's whistle!

This is the sun's doing,
these shadows
leaping, twisting,
prancing,
partners dancing
to the same tune.

CROW WONDERS

Crow knows
that hat,
that baggy coat,
that raggy ruff at the throat—
Old stuff!

The straw man
hasn't fluttered
a hand,
muttered a sound,
and the corn is sweet.

But what's
that dark thing
at his feet,
growing longer—
longer
in
the
sun?

IN THE PARK

When you've
run races
in the sun,

stolen bases,
pumped high on a
swing,

when you've
jumped Double Dutch
too much,

played

till you're
sun drunk
sun dizzy—

how shivery cool
to fling
yourself
into the tree's great
pool
of
shade.

CLACKETY CLICK

White picket fence
Boy with a stick:
Whackety crackety
Clackety
Click

Shadow boy with a stick
Shadow fence on the ground:
Shadow whack, shadow crack
Shadow clack—
Not a sound.

RECESS

The children
scribble their shadows
on the school yard,

scribble
scribble
on a great blackboard—

lanky leg
shadows
running into
lifted arm shadows
flinging
bouncing ball shapes
into skinny upside down shadows
swinging
on
long monkey bars—

till
a cloud
moving
across the morning sun
wipes out all
scribbles
like a giant
eraser.

LONG STORY

Giraffe's
shadow
moves off
in the morning light

glides over
brown brush, over
growing grass,
embraces a distant
tree

stretches its
longest-neck-in-the-world,
touches

shadows swooping,
slinking,
small shapes that
scurry

travels back,
no hurry,
settles down at
Giraffe's feet
in the high noon sun.

CLOUD SHADOW

A monster
sleeps
on a mountain—
Why?

    A monster
    cloud
    rests
    in the sky.

When the wind
blows,
and the cloud
drifts,

watch—

    below,
    the monster
    shifts,

    lifts
    its heavy head,

    opens
    its great paws
    and slips away.

BIKE RIDE

Look at us!

We ride a
road
the sun has paved with
shadows.

We glide
on leaf lace
across tree spires
over
shadow ropes
of droopy wires.

We roll
through a shade tunnel
into light.

Look!
Our bikes
spin
black-and-white
shadow
pinwheels.

WHO CAST MY SHADOW?
Three Riddles

I.

I'm lumpish,
plumpish,
your cheerful friend.
To my distress
I'm thinning,
beginning
my tearful end.
So hurry and guess.

a snowman

II.

Did an artist weave my
shadow?
So finely made am I.
My silken lines spin
orb designs—
and peril to the fly.

a spider's web

III.
A shadow bird,
I fly
Between the earth and
sky.
Great in wing and
tail
How free I seem to sail!
Not so.   *an airplane*
I cannot even move
till someone makes me go.

TELLING TIME

Time ticks,
whispers,
rings,
sounds a chime,
a ping,
a tock,
or the long slow
bong
of a grandfather clock.

Time
on the sundial
is a
shadow,
making its rounds,
moving
till day is done
in secret
understanding
with the sun.

THE FIRST

Moon,
remember
how men left their
planet
in streams of
flame,
rode weightless
in the skies
till you pulled
them down,
and then
in the blinding sunlight
how the first shadow
of an
Earthling
lay
on your
bleak dust?

THE SHADOW OF A TREE

The shadow of a
tree
can be

a willow—
hippy hair tossing
in the summer
wind

a gaunt oak in the
fall,
bereft
no leaf left

(If you're
lucky
you will see them
all)

the pine in
moonlight,
black on the snow
like a
wing,

or the shadow of
maples
not yet
solid
in the spring.

TONIGHT

Strange shadows out
tonight
in the white
light
of the moon—

shaggy humps
dark baggy bumps
meeting
darting

bat shapes
pointed heads
parting
greeting—

Strange shadows out
tonight,
all tricking and treating.

GROUND HOG DAY

Ground Hog sleeps
All winter
Snug in his fur,
Dreams
Green dreams of
Grassy shoots,
Of nicely newly nibbly
Roots—
Ah, he starts to
Stir.

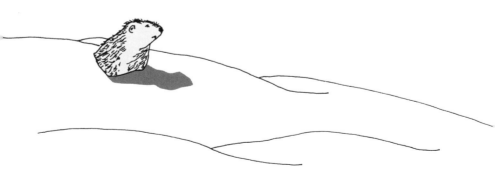

With drowsy
Stare
Looks from his burrow
Out on fields of
Snow.
What's there?
Oh no.
His shadow. Oh,
How sad!
Six more
Wintry
Weeks
To go.

ON THE WALL

On the wall,
a crocodile

See how I do it.

He thinks he's
swimming in the
Nile.

Nothing to it.

Now he has a wicked
smile

*I may rue it
Yes, I might.*

And jaws that open
half a mile . . .

*Someone PLEASE
turn out the light.*

IS THERE A PLACE?

Is there a place where
shadows go
when it is
dark?

Do they play
in the
park?
Slip down slides?

Stride down streets?
Stretch high?
Shrink thin?

Do they spin
in the wind and
fly
with leaves?

Splash in the
rain?
Hang up to
dry?

Do they miss us?
Are they
glad
to see the sun—or
sad?

37